TIPS FOR TAKING TESTS

Healthy Habits

Vicky Bureau

A Crabtree Roots Plus Book

Crabtree Publishing
crabtreebooks.com

School-to-Home Support for Caregivers and Teachers

This book helps children grow by letting them practice reading. Here are a few guiding questions to help the reader with building his or her comprehension skills. Possible answers appear here in red.

Before Reading:

- What do I think this book is about?
  - *I think this book is about how to take a test.*
  - *I think this book is about different kinds of tests.*
- What do I want to learn about this topic?
  - *I want to learn about how tests help me.*
  - *I want to learn about different types of tests.*

During Reading:

- I wonder why...
  - *I wonder why tests help me learn.*
  - *I wonder how I can prepare for tests.*
- What have I learned so far?
  - *I have learned that taking a test is a healthy habit.*
  - *I have learned that a test is a way to measure something.*

After Reading:

- What details did I learn about this topic?
  - *I have learned why tests are important.*
  - *I have learned that studying can help me prepare for some tests.*
- Read the book again and look for the vocabulary words.
  - *I see the word **measure** on page 6 and the word **prepare** on page 16. The other vocabulary words are found on page 23.*

Taking a test is a healthy **habit**.

A healthy habit is something you do to stay well.

A test is a way to **measure** something.

P D C

L P E D

P E C F D

E D F C Z P

F E L O P Z D

To measure means to learn more.

There are many kinds of tests.

Tests help others learn about us.

A doctor can test you.

This test measures your health.

A teacher can test you.

This test measures what you know.

A coach can test you.

This test measures your **skills**.

Some tests you **prepare** for.

Preparing for a test means you **study**.

Studying means reviewing what you know.

Studying can improve your **score**.

Tests help us learn more.

Taking a test is a healthy habit.

Word List

Sight Words

coach	know	something
doctor	learn	taking
healthy	many	teacher
help	more	test
improve	others	
kinds	reviewing	

Words to Know

habit

measure

prepare

score

skills

study

TIPS FOR TAKING TESTS

Healthy Habits

Written by: Vicky Bureau
Designed by: Kathy Walsh
Series Development: James Earley
Proofreader: Melissa Boyce
Educational Consultant: Marie Lemke M.Ed.

Photographs:
Shutterstock: Cover: Rido, Mochipet; pg 3 & 23 Gorodenkoff/; pg 4 paulaphoto; pg 6 & 23 karelnoppe; pg 7 karelnoppe; pg 8 Microgen; pg 10 Pressmaster; pg 11 NDAB Creativity; pg 12 wavebreakmedia; pg 13 Ground Picture; pg 14 matimix; pg 15 & 23 Stuart Monk; pg 16 & 23 Ground Picture; pg 17 & 23 sashahaltam; pg 18 chomplearn; pg 19 & 23 Tom Wang; pg 20 librakv; pg 21 Rido

Crabtree Publishing
crabtreebooks.com 800.387.7650

Printed in the U.S.A./072023/CG20230214

Published in Canada
Crabtree Publishing
616 Welland Ave
St. Catharines, Ontario
L2M 5V6

Published in the United States
Crabtree Publishing
347 Fifth Ave
Suite 1402-145
New York, NY 10016

Library and Archives Canada Cataloguing in Publication
Available at Library and Archives Canada

Library of Congress Cataloging-in-Publication Data
Available at the Library of Congress

Hardcover: 978-1-0398-0989-5
Paperback: 978-1-0398-1042-6
Ebook (pdf): 978-1-0398-1148-5
Epub: 978-1-0398-1095-2